On Ruins & Return

Also by Rachel Tzvia Back:

Poetry
Litany (Meow Press, 1995)
Azimuth (Sheep Meadow Press, 2000)
The Buffalo Poems (Duration Press, 2003)

Translations
Lea Goldberg: Selected Poetry & Drama (Toby Press, 2005)

Literary Criticism
Led by Language: the Poetry and Poetics of Susan Howe
(University of Alabama Press, 2002)

Rachel Tzvia Back

On Ruins & Return

The Buffalo Poems
(1999-2005)

Shearsman Books
Exeter

Published in the United Kingdom in 2007 by
Shearsman Books Ltd
58 Velwell Road
Exeter EX4 4LD

www.shearsman.com

ISBN-13 978-1-905700-37-0

ISBN-10 1-905700-37-7

Copyright © Rachel Tzvia Back, 2007.

The right of Rachel Tzvia Back to be identified as the author of this work has been asserted by her in accordance with the Copyrights, Designs and Patents Act of 1988. All rights reserved. No part of this publication may be reproduced, stored in a retrieval system, transmitted in any form or by any means, electronic, mechanical, photocopying, recording or otherwise, without the prior permission of the publisher.

The publisher gratefully acknowledges financial assistance for its 2005-2007 publishing programme from Arts Council England.

For my children
Daniel, Ariel and Talya

Contents

Introduction: Until we all see buffalo 9

I From Between Kastel & White Stone Quarry (1-7) 13

II On the Ruins of Palestine (8-18) 31

III Pray for the Grace of Accuracy
 – (pray for the grace of accuracy) 55
 – (the emptied house) 57
 – (soldiers on their knees in the sand) 59
 – (their sons my sons) 60
 – (scattered) 61
 – (close in their arms) 63
 – (press release) 65
 – (a dream) 67
– (After five years of writing buffalo poems) 68

IV What is Still Possible (6 Love Poems)
 – Still life 71
 – Her hands 72
 – For he who turns away 75
 – Tearing the tether 77
 – Love: fragmented 78
 – Letting me go 88

V Bringing the Buffalo Back Home 91

Notes 101
Acknowledgements 103

Until we all see buffalo

June 1999 – Jerusalem Hills (first sighting):
Because there are moments the heart waits, though it doesn't know it is waiting, at an unnamed threshold of vague contours, and it hasn't yet made out the shape of what it will be or need, or why it will be weeping, or how to hold itself from despair, all obscured in the burning air-currents of a middle-eastern midday sun. Because there are moments when every chamber of that heart listens for its own echoes (though it doesn't know it is listening), to be told it is beating as it should and to undo the great loneliness of all transitions, of distances, of violence. Because there are gifts unexpected, bundled in frayed wrappings, left as abandoned spirits on your doorstep – to be brought indoors, nursed and embraced. Quiet, at first, then growing louder: an arc of *beckoned listening* and tender answers, always uncertain, always open – an entryway back into the still-waiting heart.

A season of wildfires. The hills all scarred and blackened, sloping into changed valleys where the always sparse-in-summer vegetation is now burnt down or dusted with ash. Nothing is as it was or should be – everything shifted with the fires, earth and animal and birds who now have nowhere to perch. Paths that once led to fragrant spring or deep well swerve in jagged blackened stones and lead one astray. I am driving home, almost sundown – mother of sons, pregnant now with a daughter. She lies inside me horizontally, refuses to turn her head down – we both wait. On the curving road between severed hills, I stop –

must stop, the road is spinning, will not settle. I step out of the car, crouch by the side of the road, put my head between my knees for a moment until the nausea passes. When I raise my eyes toward the vast silence of the charcoaled gnarled hills, I see it.

There, where the slope meets valley floor, as though it had just stepped out from behind the charred wings, unwedded to the broad stage, shifting the balance – all

eyes (my eyes) to the far corner, to the hulking mass in a crevice of space, in shimmering still smoke-tinged air –

a buffalo.

Still, erect, frozen. Silent. Its thick furred hair motionless in the windless air. Its hump its own solitary mountain, carried from far-away places. Its head half-lowered, in profile – a dark brown buffalo, wandered into these Jerusalem hills.

Israel (*Jacob's terrain*), Palestine, Canaan, Palesti'na (*land of strangers*), Judea, Holy Land. All, and none of the above. No name fits. Every name too beautiful and too narrow. Every name too desirous of sovereignty (where wild hills nightly wander off to visit distant sisters, return by daybreak, their white stones telling the tale to anyone who will listen). Land (he said) fatally embraced by the deity. Land that punishes itself and all who love it (too much); land that is punished by all who love it (too much). Land that is my home. Here, where there were never buffalo – but here

it is.

I watch it. I wait for it to move (which it does not). I want it to look at me (which it does not). Cars behind me speed their way to the capital, but I do not hear them – I am immersed, deep in a silent embrace, in the space and stillness between us, in everything it carries in its unwieldy shape: dark peace and darker pain.

I watch it – this wandered-from-far buffalo – for a minute or an hour, until the muezzin calls, until the baby turns, until the last light slips away and I can no longer distinguish its form from the black hills, or from the burnt valley.

January 1, 2000 – from Mount Scopus (an interim):
The baby girl is six-months old. The buffalo is mostly forgotten. And this night, bundled in blankets and drinking black coffee, looking out toward the still-in-darkness desert, we are all waiting for first rays of the new millennium. Perched on this mountaintop facing east, strangers and friends, we want to believe – so, we have convinced ourselves of false things. We choose not to see. The baby girl has blue eyes we say are from far seas – the desert too (we say) promises fertility and blossoms, and we watch the first tinge of pink creep over the ridge, the baby's soft soft cheeks cool in the pre-dawn breeze. The light spreads slowly, first slender golden arms stretching, gentle awakenings, as the sky's darkness gradually retreats. And when the first shy sun of the year 2000 finally appears over the desert mountains, everyone cheers.

October 2000 – the Galilee/the Occupied Territories
First or final insult. Every insult and wound in between. Wound of what is wrenched away, of wrestled will that can bear no more. We (Israelis) are ignorant. When the first riot erupts, we fail to understand. Fires reach our doorstep, and still we fail to see. In the rage and flames, the ripped-out street-lamps, the young boys shouting in the village square, the roads blocked with burning tires, the riot police shooting into the crowd – in the rage and flames, I remember the buffalo. By riots' end, thirteen (Palestinian-Israeli) Galilean boys are dead. So the second uprising begins. The streets are soon bloody (Ramallah, Jenin, Sachnin, Jerusalem, Tel-Aviv, Gaza, and again demolished Jenin). The ledgers are quickly filled with the names of children. My three grow strong, as though they are safe. Hearts close, and then seal shut. I remember the buffalo, and a heart waiting (to be opened). From that moment, it stays with me, wanders through my days, carrying the weight of the violence on its broad back, in its vast and silent eyes – and it allows me to write

what I could not have otherwise.

I From Between Kastel & White Stone Quarry

1 *(Palimpsest of place)*

Swell of hills across Judea

        stretch
            to open clear
                between peaks where
sky

        slips lower
            into smooth cols –
                down slender neck, as sweat
                    in crook of a collarbone –
sloped stunted shrubs
        half-burnt trees or absent
                trees

        coal dust on gnarled
            thornbushes, their tufted centers
                thick in place of
and the air
        parched

edges curling inward like bleached and
                      brittle parchment

                here, in midday
                    mid-range
at footslip on incline
        where stones scattered
                are white markings
to nowhere

in the bright glare of rays deflecting
                what I believe
            I see
        deeper into first sighting

            a dark and heavy shape
move

                 a buffalo

              wandered far from white
     cedar hickory red-berried hawthorne wild and ice
laced
              curled horns downturned
                    head he carries low
         cannot raise but to shoulder level I think
                  I see his body
heave
        in this heat in this wavering
                  air under the weight
                        of this wide flame-white eastern
   sky

On American plains there were once
                          sixty million, here
      there were none

        though now I see him   here
              as though returning
                        remnant

              (dark thick-tongued ruminant
              massive beast of crowded herds)

                     his solitary ruins
        to this narrowland
still brown body
       in still and dry heat
                suspended

The scene should be framed and hung on walls as

        is, as
            from anywhere
                in these hills –
          highpitch of air punctured –
single shot
      in perfect flight through will
           pierce fur
                flesh and he too
                        will fall

        another small
              soon
                  indistinct
                        dark decomposing

      heap
            as ancient and pointless
                      as the rest

2

The past I didn't choose
that is mine.

The desire unwieldy and wide
in a body disobeying

again and a mind clouded
down. A doubt,

ruined metal rooted
at a roadside along the rush of cars,

the unrelenting rust taste at the tongue's edges
that will not lift with water – doubt

in a place of stonesteady
believers. Always misnamed, he is

this: what wakes
when I wake, wherever I wake,

what sleeps when I do, he is
what walks when I walk, his weight

the lead-marrow in my bones
singed and spiked branding on my legs,

longings, words. He is what I dream,
the black ropes

that will not hold, the blood
that flows unnoticed though the dirt

stained darker smells of fresh
kill, he is the someone,

something of broad uncertain shape,
dragging a broken self

into these jagged hills, my always
foreign horizon.

3

From my home between ruined
kastel and white stone

quarry where waiting
is skies blind and silent

blue but for the breathing
that swells like a bruise where

waiting is just
waiting

the return of children
the returning of bodies

back from somewhere else
nearby

blown up pieces scattered
wide across a marketplace

blood stain
two-stories high

or pieces
piled up on a ridge in a dark

border crossing night
Quarry was the heart

gouged out and fed
to the hounds, quarry was

a place of stone incessant
drilling

to nowhere but dust
and emptied crater the quarry

was a heap of dead bodies
If back then the buffalo

had just lain down not
raced beside trailing smoke black

tracks dark indifferent
trains that stormed

across open spaces to slash
a gold quiet

in two and their thick-furred breathing
wet with fear and phlegm

beneath black clouds, black
shotguns slanting from the windows

to pick them off one by one, easiest aim as
they kept pace

with the trains and if
they had just

lain down in the dirt
if they had

just
stopped

then or here
where there is nothing

left
but blankets of dust

4

> *"The prairies are covered with the carcasses of bison."*
> *The New York Times*, 4 April 1880

When the herds still darkened the plains.

Millions passed through
stretching north to south 100 miles   *It is no mere animal. It is*
a single moving mass 7-8 miles deep.   *the sun's shadow.*

The scouts came first crossing   *If it lives, we live. If it dies,*
forbidden territory riding into   *we die. It is our life, our*
their midst and the giant beasts   *living shield.*
grazing in the draws gently
parted paving a way   *Chief Quanah Parker*
for the men on their horses then   *Chief Stone-Cave-Son Wild-*
wave to breathing wave   *Horse Serpent-Scales Slue-Foot*
closed seamlessly behind them.   *Coyote*

The grass was lush, the animals   *Spotted-Feather Wolf-Tongue*
fat from spring abundance.   *Satanta Soft-Foot*
The bulls' shaggy manes announced   *Stone-Teeth*
afternoon winds and their   *Medicine Man Isatai*
demise. At sundown, the buffalo   *Hiram Watson Sam Smith Fred*
shadows grew long and lean.   *Leonard "Shorty" Shadler*
The great slaughter began at dawn.   *Billy "Dutch" Tyler*

It was the winter of 1872-73.   *Henry Mike Welch*
The air thick with blood and dead   *Mrs. William Olds*
buffalo Bestiary with no moral.

Hind quarters taken first the rest left   *All dead at Adobe Walls battle*
to spoil Hides added later to the prize.
In Wright & Rath's warehouse it was   *and the buffalo in the canyons*
no uncommon thing (the newspapers
noted) to see 60 to 80,000 buffalo   *set out a path of escape cross*

hides stretched flat for travel east piled   a threshold unmarked   She
high dark-skinned mountains. Wright   still waits for news of
himself boasted a killing of 22,000.   you

Those who escaped the bullet escaped   beyond the wall at
little every sip of water every mouthful   the farthest edge
of grass at risk of life miserable   of today's killings
animals driven far from their haunts
as hunters continued relentless pursuit.   You went to protect protest
In the end they rendered no tallow   claim undo sanctify settle
(wrote a Nebraska rancher) only stringy
meat the few remaining ones run   survive
almost to death.

1880, space redefined for their absence: in the fleeting light
"I have traveled over a thousand miles
across the plains," wrote the stunned
westward traveler, "and I must tell you   find home
I am never out of sight of a dead
buffalo, never in sight
of a live one."

          Forgive me, I was mistaken.

          In this forsaken country where I searched
          for myself
          I will never be found.

          If you see anyone bound out here pray
          warn them

          Dearest – I am
          yours

          until we all see buffalo.

5 *(no name or mane)*

It is the soul
suddenly

      wandering off

           like a butterfly
or a buffalo:

      it is

         soul-loss

      Frayed red string round the wrist
cannot keep it tied
to body

      to me

canst thou bind the buffalo with his band
      in the furrow? or will he harrow
                the valleys
  after thee

      who is now sadness
               and sickness –

If
      it comes back
           I'll get well
I've been told

      but the names I call

         re'em
    anoa

                        tamarau
            carabao cape wild
                        bovidae or
        bison

                    furred words
lumbering forth from
            gray-tinged skies
                        final pre-storm
rays, chill even at this distance

        are all wrong

How then to call
                the lost soul
back

I would follow it
                wordless

into what valley
who

    hath, as it were
the strength
        of the buffalo?

            but am stopped

            body stripped
left behind:

        breathing carcass

6

Like the red-starred
        ambulance
                which raced
through city streets
        beyond city

limits with siren and lights flashing
        toward the child

fallen

    wingless, windless

            from a jagged
        rooftop

broken on stones below
        three-year old body still

breathing   barely
                and the ambulance
at village entrance
        stopped .

    sweet bird beside the buffalo, both
motionless

Like
    the ambulance with white
            smoke trails

from exhaust

        metal hot
    in the late cool afternoon
        where children play

high
       voices
              carried away
by last light of
       all setting suns

where an ambulance
           has stopped
                  at the road-block

at the village entrance
                 waits
for army escort

toward the child
       meters away

breath now *bird* threaded air

ambulance unmoved before
                  the alley rising rushing toward
     the pleading uncles
promising safety in
       the now uncertain
                  dusk grey

light where the ambulance waits
                  its unwieldy
shape
       idling

    the buffalo deaf and still
    in hills crouching low
    before mourning houses

7 *(And when you see Jerusalem)*

in her shade of scarred
    stone walls around stone
        homes roads hills in her
storm of stones thrown from ancient lookouts
    with stone-sacred certainty and stone
        memories placed gently
on stone tombs

And when you see that city that
    Jerusalem her open squares covered
        with rocks tossed hurled
pitched at moving targets the ground on which
    we would stand unevenly stitched
        patchwork of protest
and prayer-frenzy

When you see that Jerusalem
    encompassed by those who love
        her history of boulders still unearthed
and her history of exposed rocks hoarding the sun's
    winter warmth when you see that Jerusalem
        encompassed by those who
love her

More than life more than the lives
    of their sons and daughters
        my sons and daughter
who sleep in warm rooms their cheeks flushed
    skin sweaty and sweet as they
        sleep in this pale safety
that will not last

When you see Jerusalem
    surrounded by the armies
        of those who love her too much

love her weight her warmth her steadfast bulk immobile
       behemoth in moonlight her promised
              permanence engraved
in the stones

They love too much –

    Then flee – flee to the mountains.

II On the Ruins of Palestine

8

I live on the ruins of Palestine

Slow to speech thick
        of tongue quick
      in anger ancient
parched
              fear

      In the ruins on a land
through a night
              ignited

      By a single
            singed vision
and another
      single spark

Cradled close in a charred palm
    chiseled in a stonedream
          carried across history

Through the dark beneath our bare
                          feet

Strangers all

On the ruins of Palestine

9

Saplings on the hillside
>   first to burn

Most slender most eager and frailest
>   hope

Eastern straw winds
>   sweep flames across our
>   dislodged doorstep

Into a spoken first-fire
>   first-command:

Take of the water of the river, pour it
>   *upon the dry land; and the water*
which you take out of the river shall
>   *become blood.*

The bush unconsumed all-
>   consuming   my child
>   hot with fever

>   cannot hold his head up
>   to see
>   fires
>   beneath his bed
>   room window (wandering
> white buffalo

>   frozen in flamelight
>   behind our clenched eyes –
>   imagined marker
>   of near-by
>   water)

"Blessed is she
      who in her lifetime has seen
                    the most water"

Who has seen has not seen
              blessed is she

10 *(a fable and a nursery rhyme)*

The children were missing limbs
In the southern sand region they
were missing:
a leg a foot an arm
I sent my northern children out looking

The moon was full the paths were white
night
was smooth just the ripple
of my children's high voices
skipping stones in the dry wadis:
> Hunter horn berry and bird,
> Hunter horn berry and fish.
> Hunter clover nut and bird,
> Whisper a secret, make a wish.

Daniel led the way said
he was unafraid and held
his brother's hand
Beneath an olive tree they stopped
to eat treats I had packed and to play
echoes and acorns
> Hunter horn berry and bird,
> Tell me, child, what have you heard?
> The sky at sunset is redder than red
> And buffalo-robes will be your bed.

In the southern sand region
under starched white sheets
the children reached
for missing legs that ached
and called to them
to leave the fevered body behind
> Hide and seek in buffalo-clover,
> You'll wake up child, when the hunt is over.

> Hunter horn berry and bird,
> Tell me no more of what you have heard.

My children went looking for
limbs the other children would no longer need
My beautiful children came back
flushed
empty-handed

[Kfar Darom Settlement, Gaza – Nov. 2000: A Palestinian bomb is detonated on a road as a school bus drives by. The two adults on the bus are killed, 5 children are wounded. Three children from one family all lose their limbs.]

11

When we no longer care
       who or how many
are dead
        our own
      running through sprinklers
         in the still
               ablaze
afternoon

when we are too weary
        too hot too bored
            to read even
one more name or
     that day's favorite
tale:

two teenage daughters dead in a day

two bodies on two stretchers
             and their mother
    fallen upon them   her mouth
                   mangled in open agony
as she strokes their lovely long legs
      now covered in flags

              one more bomb
in a season of many

when we cannot remember the name
     of the smallest baby girl

             carried through narrowstreets
amid crowds of mourners
     curled in her father's arms she is
        tiny

slightest bundle
       of cloth bread wild
              wildflowers
in her father's arms

carried to the graveyard to the crumbling
       edge of driest dirt
              in a season of stray
      bullets

              no one claims someone
                         aimed

when we count our days
       by which bloody "incident"
              killed whose children
in what village or city
       while we travel
              to work
and back home
       and we no longer care

so long as our own
       can still run through sprinklers
                   in the late-afternoon
blazing
       heat

12 *(the Still Hunt)*

Conceals himself a hundred
        yards upwind in a wallow
                or behind
the rise in bluff where
        he marks the lead cow
                at perfect center
of cross-sights (cross-bones cross-
        love

hung high from a
        bleached-white tree)

She
    will not lead them now
                away from danger   He
has named first shot for her
        aimed first shot
                below her shoulder bone
to rip into darkshelter dry
        echo
            of her lungs
where breath rushes out
                will not return

Bewildered
        she drops to one foreleg then
                to the other kneeling
in dust we are kneeling in dust
        what do you
                hear
what does the herd
        hear

A rifle's rupture of space
                across river ravine

    ruminants and the land
          at last stampeding
              as again

we take aim

13 *(what has anchored us)*

The ballast of their breathing
                    in the next room in the bed
beside in the darkened house
            enchanted
                        breath expanding

to the rhythm of our fantasy:
                    buffalo stars
stampeding through
            unblemished skies
above a sacred land we imagined
                            our own

 The weight of the unwritten
                        truth
 at well-bottom: rabid fear
            perched on the back of the absent
 buffalo

The certainty of migrating cormorants
            in massive flocks their flight
                        path and patterns
absolute: they return every year
      to rest here

in the Huleh valley around the reflooded
     swamp of the north   where
I walk   October 2001
       one year after
             the women of Sachnin first

buried their faces
            in the rough wind-dried still
                        sweet smelling clothes of their
dead sons

14

October 2001   twenty years after
      I first returned   Now
in the marshy valley at red
      mountain's foot   at dusk:

A still life in the spectrum's
      every noble colour: indigo
    and scarlet reign the returned
lake   reeds and sedge rooted

in water thick and crowded the canvas
      lit from behind with brightest
whitewash   Time still in a perfect
      porcelain bowl   my sons

transfixed at lake's edge
    by shifting shadows of the huge
      water buffalo   hiding in the bush
and by the birds   frozen in flight

their dark V marking the fragile sky their
    perfect hearts my frightened heart
      just before they wing
out of sight

15

But they are extinct   extinguished
    flame fire flushed color
of cheek
        favored child you would   (in another's world)

could   could not protect
        (you crouch together for cover)

        or the blue-eyed father moving
south on a besieged road to bring
        his soldier son home

drives into a daylight ambush   death
    rises from the roadside shadows
he can see it race towards him

        between first bullet and last
            son home hope
    are left waiting

there is no bringing him back

there is no bringing them back

    the buffalo

their bellowing thirst in the then
    dried swamp still distinct
  in a quiet dusk

    and their shadow:

last stagger of a memory

            or is it

    this late-afternoon crimson light
and the lies

    we continue to tell ourselves

16 *(April invasion)*

What stands between us
impenetrable

Lumbered from distances
ice-crystals still in hooves

Tracks tars tanks
rumbling where starred

Roads made ragged ribbed
chests bared ammunition

Residue on hearts inside
beating

Horns of bone cannon metal
covered in dust down

Dirt paths blind blind alleys
demolished walls

Reveal eyes all I
can see crushed cinder-blocks

Concrete cement and stone
hearts beating

Beating dark fur red rugs
still draped by gaping holes

Herd a heap heard the whole
loss lost

To bodies left in the rain
rot in the sun

Will no one cover console
carry them away

They are evidence
of what was

Here home school street
what has

Obscured the beloved's face
and I hear a heart

whose
voice like my own

is asking:
How fast can you bury your dead?

17

What stands between us
a girl

Her hair black long
her eyes

Lovely.
This is not suicide

she says
in the grainy video-taped

interview This is
Sacrifice

Selfless spirit to sustain
Hope Kill

as many as she
can this beautiful human

bomb I've been told
How the Buffalo stepped forward

during the time of famine
Worship

its selflessness they say
with explosive belt strapped

around her belly she looked
Pregnant

she looked lumbering larger
than one self

in a moment the moment before
deafening stops up time

and space with nails bolts glass
splinters what is left is

mangled
metal blood flesh

to be scraped off the street
collected in sandwich bags

so the whole the whole
can be buried

whole:
Howl!

O gates; Cry, O City!
The whole

of Palestina
is dissolved into tears

of mourning.

18 *(dispossessed)*

Drought of years
duration

Longer than any

In memory than any
memory

Beneath   On a slope
Blackhills Judith   of Olive
Ridge Highwood   trees wild Mint

Mountains   Myrrh Anise red
Sioux and Arapahoes   Anemone the people
on short-grass plains   of Mi'ar

in search of search for   in search of search for
forage last Herds   Markings
the stories solitary   of former homes

White Buffalo   razed after the War
who will lead them   and the Well
to water   where it once stood

I am writing this
unrooted

In the moment
before

Stampede to the bluff

Fire behind us
Alongside us

And ahead

Where escarpment ends
Our wild plunge

into Sweet untouched air

III Pray for the Grace of Accuracy

♦ *(pray for the grace of accuracy)*

Words repeated
until they lose all meaning

Once it was
desert desire dream

but the sand image failed
the dune was death the desire

dark fragments
one would not own

as own in daylight
woven too tight with

submission
power none of it is

as imagined *dream*
emptiest of all

for its bottomless nature for its
brash foolishness

Now
I want to disallow

mangled howl severed
limbs lean and curved

shapes on the page sounds
in my mouth

that say too little claim
to know but finally

stand empty
the hollowed heart

*harrowed art
can never be*

silent even when
empty as empty

as an emptied house

◆ *(emptied house)*

Outside the emptied house

there were soldiers on their knees

in the sand

sifting for body parts moving

forward in a line they

crawled inch by inch through

sand gravel glass and weeds

wild with metal splinters

in search of lost slivers

flesh skin nails smallest

drops of not-yet dried blood

that would have been brothers

blown up on patrol jeep and men

vanished

into thin air this is no

smoke and mirrors magic trick

nothing left

resembling the human

but soldiers on their knees

in the sand

♦   *(soldiers on their knees in the sand)*

Grandfather who cut his nails
every Friday

before sunset and before his peaceful
Sabbath queen arrived

would save the pale slivers in a box
to be buried with him

Dust unto dust he said
with not a single particle missing

The dream was of the day
the dead would rise

whole
in the next world

mothers watching
soldiers on their knees

sifting and searching for body parts
do not think of next worlds

they think only of
lost worlds:

their sons my sons
the setting sun

building tunnels and towers
in the sand

♦   *(their sons my sons)*

Lost limbs again
    this time in a strawberry field

Early morning January sun rises
    gently talks softly to yesterday's
        rain lingering still at field's edge

where perfect strawberries are ready for eating
    first day of the feast festival of the sacrifice
        Ishmael taken to the hilltop Issac carried away

This time it is mother Maryam who does not know
    the boys her boys woke early to a school-less day
        they are racing now through the strawberry field

The red fruit is full sweet with dew and dawn is
    collecting night's blankets day is waiting to spread her
        arms around us all in the fields and the boys cannot

say how or from where there was no sign a bomb would fall
    in the early morning family field the boys do not know
        their legs are bleeding their bodies lie still their

limbs are scattered they are half-boys and dead boys
    none of them know how later before the funerals after
        the hospital Maryam will return to the charred and
            beautiful

bleeding strawberry field
    to gather in her scarf scattered flowers
        and flesh

[Gaza, Jan. 2005: An Israeli bomb is dropped on 12 boys in a strawberry field. 7 boys are killed; the five survivors all lose limbs.]

♦ (*scattered*)

Like salt or sand
    dispossessed of the sea   strands
        of a story stolen away

like stars
    in steep and black chords   abandoned
        to distant skies

    the silent eye
  cannot see   tents in the snow
        tossed like white loaves

  on still waters
no miracle   mother   memory
    wrapped in blanket or braid

not lost

            Call them home
        call them in
one by one   tender ones

to sit down
    to dinner   together
      before

light fades

on burning stone
    red poppy wild almond blossom   before

hills drop their coral robes

      walk naked into night
    holding small bodies

like stars
      close in their arms

◆   *(close in his arms)*

The black stone Gabriel carried
to earth

(his wings trembling still
from the great weight)

flawless black planes
smoother than palms in caress

softened by veneration hardened
by desire

Into the granite valley she travels

Hajj holy journey
sister who was once

the left-behind baby
now into the dust valley

She carries a flag

On it imprinted her brother's
face favored eldest she never knew

now
unnumbered silent miles

from unforgiving lands still ravaged
to meet him in Mecca

a promise
carried by courier a plan possibility

for strangers siblings two pilgrims
among two million

around the sacred Ka'aba

She holds her flag high She
is faith

in brothers she never met will never

This her final march toward the solitary
maned and maimed animal

of the alone

Howling in every lost
home heart she

stands apart
in this tale

which is not mine to tell

but I tell it

◆   (press release)
                    January 26th 2004

Nobody was killed in al Nabi Saleh tonight

Only

500 old and young

forced to stand hours in the cold

in the middle of night

in the rain

in the range

of snipers on the watchtower

and the children

in flannel pajamas with coats thrown over
*   thick in layers too loose and bulky to hold*
*   sweet calves baby buffalo   their feet pushed*
hurried
*   into shoes without socks their small finger bones cold*
*   as clay brittle in their parents' hands their*
faces
*   still soft in sleep but eyes waking would be*
*   eager or earnest now pulled to screeching jeeps and*
*   wild searchlights scattering sharp-cut*
lightbeams
*   like diamond treasures dreams in the dark*
megaphones calling out calling names cutting
*   silence into strips and coloring their racing hearts*
crayon black

in the middle of the night

in the rain

in the range

of snipers

the children

thinking they dream

♦ (*a dream*)

The burnt-out bus carcasses
        reared their mangled heads
and started to howl.

At every death site   every intersection
        across the city   metal jagged
scorched black glass

splinters for eyes limbs scattered low
        and high between the seats under unimagined
ache of ancient beasts.

One curled around a stilled body   held it
        close like the baby who just finished
crying *there* *there*

the holding the touching the tender
        place of nestled after all the while
the bloody buses

across the city   howling   and in my dream
        I knelt down beside the tender one
and begged it

to make room for me too.

♦   *After five years of writing buffalo poems*

I wondered what had happened to the buffalo.

One day she was gone   disappeared
from the page

There had been a moment of *beckoned listening*
on a charred hillside   where I found her   no   she
found me though   she never made a sound   only
my heart   heard her stillness in the wadi   and the heavy

haze   crackled with the slight hum of her curved back its
furred arch   pushing upward against the unforgiving
sky   pregnant threats in the air   it was rounded
like a woman's lovely belly   as though a baby could push

out of her back   into the day   a different day   unmaimed un
named   by fire or fear: fierce athena in full armour   glorious
goddess   out of zeus' aching forehead   readying for peace   how
I long for her   she could protect

my children   athena *adina*   guard my sister's health   her shield
glows in the midday middle-east   sunblinds   soldiers freedom
fighters terrorists generals   slowly   she raises her arms   have you
seen the leafless oak tree at incline   its branches luminous

with hope   in the wadi   the buffalo   imagined dark baby beast
trudged off   I didn't even notice   until she was gone   and I
kept calling   as though in her name   there was a moment   but
not mine to keep   now   I write buffalo poems

in her absence

IV What is Still Possible

(6 Love Poems)

Still life
        with children

Three
    intertwined on the floor

Her head on his belly her hair light
    rivulets cross his chest the moon-born
        middle one wrestles in their midst one
moment studies his cards the next three alone
    together they are
        what will be

left later what will remain after what
    each can count on when   and then
        she giggles he tickles
her chest and the middle one brings
    treats from the kitchen

three of a kind
    put out on the floor   hearts
        diamonds and spades
fade

into what will be their past   and then
    their future
        without me

Her hands

Her hands
open on her lap
empty and

motionless
palms facing up
as in

prayer pale
lines leading
nowhere

and a ragged
lifeline
that tells

one great lie
Littlest
spirit she

carried and
could not
protect

from what
from whom
in the darkened

warm room where
baby breaths
hovered

promising
themselves
in the narrow and

precarious
world
suddenly

gone
The debate
as to how

or if
one recovers
raging in whispers

in every corner
beside the empty
stroller above

the empty
crib
within

emptied
terrified hearts
and she

is as
small
as still

and silent
as the baby girl
who was

tenderly rocked
to sleep
and then

never
woke up

To he who turns away

from arms open
to embrace

consider
the heart that sounds

a sudden desire in life's
common moment

unexpected unasked
arrives

in white pink all
hues

in between
of almond blossomings

that wild-without-warning
roadside rapture

to stay
who knows how long

moments or days
the babies'

soap soft skin
fragrance

you thought
would never end

where does it
intoxicate now

while you might walk
through open doors

into an open heart
toward what is

still possible

Tearing the tether

The sadness of something lost   nothing
that was mine

I am   refused   he wants
refuge

from desire   not possible
I want to tell him   it is

the deluge
as promised   delivered   that day

today   tomorrow
if the gods love you   but he

holds in hand   the docile
dove   the one

who will not fly   wild
over changing terrains   as first dark

and glorious storm   begins
or ends   and though this day too

descends
and I would tear the tether   set out

to swelling sea   still
he will not kiss me.

Love: fragmented

♦ *(the heart)*
cleft, as in
divided

the rift between
what was spoken

and what sits
silent

in a corner
unattended

aching

♦ *(the child)*
always enters
the room

just as you might
turn

toward the door
listening

for another's footsteps
she

enters the room
insistent and

demanding
you see she's been

crying

◆ *(rain)*
unannounced
though awaited

ragged summer long
scorched

everything even
singed

desire
now stirs

in the rain
in the hills

where I walk
and you

at a distance
cannot say why now

you weep
waging war

with absence
you cannot name

though
your eyes

far-away islands
are greener

for the sorrow

♦ *(land)*
that would be
my body

for you
alone at sea

a place
to wash up on

steady still
until

you graze
unsteady

against it
touch lips

to my breasts
soft

silkweed foreign
milkweed

monarch
lifts off the flower

a landscape
shifts

will not settle
rifts –

the damage is done

◆ *(millstone)*
because every desire
met

opens to another
because

there are forms of torture
the gods

never thought of because
a boulder

sits on your chest
a stone

in my mouth
while you pull

away wanting silence
imagining

escape

◆ *(the child, again)*
fourth in the family
forgotten she is

sitting on the edge
of a balcony

she has black hair
she is blond as wheat

your dark lashes
green eyes

she is yours
she is

me
collecting words

in blank notebooks
pins them to the page

stilled butterflies because
she is ruthless

stronger than I
will ever be

I long to know her
and then

leave her far behind

◆ *(ruthless)*
you pin my arms
to my sides

savaged self
you are

looking to salvage
something

you never knew
you needed

you move
inside

fierce
candlelight

shadows stir
something

untamed
twigs and tinder

into fire
on a dry and wild

mountainside bare
or brutal when

pleased my need
grows hiding

your own in guarded
gardens

hedges high
(the fire dies)

you turn to go

◆ *(in the garden)*
she was bereft
the heart

broken
cleft leaf

when she moved
to embrace him

he pushed her away
don't cleave to me

he said
don't

pierce or penetrate
don't

tear open apart
don't

need or seek
an embrace don't

hold to

◆ *(two languages)*
left to right right
to left

they might
meet

in the middle
but rarely do

letters
nothing alike   yours

tender like you
austere like you

angular   ancient
having traveled distances

and deserts
(when you speak

there is sand gravel
in your throat)

my letters rounded
curved   cursed

with youth
surrounding

emptiness
in the gap

between the two
how often

do we fall

♦ *(into silence)*
with every kiss your
tongue

touching mine
you swallow

another word
steal

what was mine
until

I am
wordless

would
there be love

in a wordless
world

in the night
by the crescent

I can see
the almond tree

blooming in perfect
wordless

white
undisturbed

by silence
but I

reach for a branch
your bare

arm
any sound or

syllable
something

unsevered
unbroken

as if your word
of love

could hold me
whole

in the world

Letting me go

at water's edge the doe
is feeding

she hears me come near
she has

no fear her ears
sharpen as she

holds my gaze we
are still

all these years
later

watching
the water flow

together
faster now

as the children
grow there was

no knowing
in the beginning

we could trust
the storms

that stunned and spoke
our angry

hearts – they too
would feed

the necessary flow
pulling downstream

the doe
wanders off

hart's-tongue
left behind

ever undivided
do you know

I would starve
without you

and today's sun
stitching gold

into the water is you
far away

letting me go
knowing

I will always
come home.

V Bringing the Buffalo Back Home
(October 2005, Adirondacks NY)

◆

I brought the buffalo back
home

Sacred and scarred
harbored afar   she

had wandered across
continents

white corded waters
into roped-off histories

onto forgotten minefields
where poppies bloom

every spring in wild red
rings around a dark unseeing eye

in foolish memory
of the boys

who once lay there
bleeding their search

for lost lamb
or glinting valley

mystery
of last night's dream

aborted midglory
She too

had scaled fence and border
disregarded

warning markers
to stand

among the parched and burnt
in a bloody valley

silent defiance inhuman
will ancient form

the gifts from here
and there

I first saw her there
she first stole

the image
broke open lies

shattered quartz
crenellated fear

spoke a quiet
hope kept

me company
until

one day
she was gone –

I had no choice:
alone

I brought her
home

to this amber autumn
crimson

the canvas
across a rain-swollen stream

accents of desire and absolute
surrender

in the falling leaves winter
waiting

at water's edge
in white vapor rising

faintest fragrance of ice
and snow

promising
she may still lose herself

for a season
in thick fur

and forgetfulness
One must have memories

he wrote, *and then*
one must forget them. One must

have vast patience
until they come

again, and when
they become blood

within us, glance and gesture,
then

it may happen
in a rare hour

the first word of a verse
the first

pulse of a heart
opened *ardent*

for another
may arise

———————

I brought my heart's buffalo home

to a long night's lodging
cradled caress

in candle-light
silence of eyes

that can conceive
of love

where unallowed
Brought her home

to the wooded hillside
where hidden

among wet and trembling
leaves *love*

a single boulder
(unwieldy bulk

of all ancient beasts)
loomed high linked

earth to a lonely sky
and an equally lonely god

was perched at boulder's edge
waiting to be found

Brought her home because
in the sounding beat

of what felt
broken

she spoke
a measure of land

that is a soul's own
though you seek refuge

in first households
forfeited long ago

Brought her home
No

she brought herself
back home

beautiful acolyte
of ancient lands

holy and promised
promises

broken now
decaying leaves

underfoot rustling
like the faded

leaves
of first dark books

where her exile
my anger

took hold
Home

already then a place
haunted

by what
is untold She

taught me to tell
and in the end

she lumbered off
into that unsettled quiet

of an early morning
gathering storm

I saw her leave
My

solitary heart
did not weep

as I knew
this is exactly

as it should be.

Notes

Introduction: Until we all see buffalo
"*beckoned listening*" is from Hank Lazer's *The New Spirit* (Singing Horse Press, 2005), p.16.

"land fatally embraced by the deity" is from Herman Melville's "Is the desolation of the land the result of the fatal embrace of the Deity? Hapless are the favorites of Heaven" – in *Journal Up the Straits: October 11, 1856-May 5, 1857* (Cooper Square Publishers, 1971), p.92.

"land that punishes itself and all who love is" is from Dennis Silk's *Argument* in his book *The Punished Land* (Penguin Books, 1980), p. 61. Silk writes: "These poems are about a land too beautiful for its inhabitants. So they punished it (or rather her) with a general ill will. […] Perhaps she's also a punishing land. She's called Palestine because it's her best name."

I From Between Kastel & White Stone Quarry (1-7)
4 "When the herds still darkened the plains" is taken from Charles G. Anderson's *In Search of the Buffalo: The Story of J. Wright Mooar* (Pioneer Press, 1996), p. 16. Information about "the great buffalo slaughter" and the battle at Adobe Walls, including the names of the dead, is taken from this same book, pages 18-64.

5 (no name or mane)
Title: "*no name or mane*" is from Susan Howe's *Pythagorean Silence* in *The Europe of Trusts* (Sun & Moon Classics, 1990), p.25.

Lines 12-15: "*canst thou bind/ the buffalo with his band in the furrow? or will he harrow/ the valleys/ after thee*" – Cf. Job 39:10.

Lines 41-44: "*who/ hath as it were/ the strength/ of the buffalo*" – Cf. Numbers 24:22.

7 (when you see Jerusalem)
Title and final line: Cf. Luke 21:20-21 – "And when you see Jerusalem surrounded by armies, then you will know that the time of its destruction has arrived. Then those in Judea must flee to the hills. Let those in Jerusalem escape . . ."

II On the Ruins of Palestine (8-18)
9
Lines 10-13: "*Take of the water of the river, pour it/ upon the dry land; and the water/ which you take out of the river shall/ become blood*" – Cf. Exodus 4:9.

17
Final lines: "*Howl! / O gates*" – Cf. Isaiah 14: 31: "Howl, O gate; cry, O city; thou, whole Palestina art dissolved: for there shall come from the north a smoke, and none shall be alone in his appointed times."

III Pray for the Grace of Accuracy
♦ (*pray for the grace of accuracy*)
Title is taken from Robert Lowell's poem 'Epilogue'.

IV What is Still Possible
Love: fragmented
In the section "*(in the garden)*", italicized "*don't cleave to me*" – Cf. The Gospel According to St. John, 20:17.

V Bringing the Buffalo Back Home
Italicized lines "*One must have memories . . .*" until "*the first word of a verse*" and "*may arise*" are from Rainer Maria Rilke, *Malte* pp.25-27, quoted by C.F. MacIntyre in his introduction to *Rilke: Selected Poems* (University of California Press, 1966).

Acknowledgements

Grateful acknowledgment is made to the editors of the following literary journals where some of these poems first appeared: *Bridges: A Jewish Feminist Journal*, *Ensemble Jourine*, *The Drunken Boat*, *Golden Handcuffs Review*, *Sulfur* and *A View from the Loft*. Special gratitude is owed to Jerrold Shiroma of Duration Press for publishing *The Buffalo Poems* chapbook.

It is with abundant gratitude that the author acknowledges The Blue Mountain Center and its devoted staff for providing the time, peace and exquisite setting necessary to complete this book. It was those weeks at Blue Mountain that helped bring the buffalo back home.

www.ingramcontent.com/pod-product-compliance
Lightning Source LLC
Chambersburg PA
CBHW031159160426
43193CB00008B/434